The Very Hungover Caterpillar

This book has not been prepared, approved, licensed or endorsed by any entity involved in the creation or production of *The Very Hungry Caterpillar* including Penguin Books Ltd. and Eric Carle LLC.

CONSTABLE

First published in Great Britain in 2014 by Constable

A CIP catalogue record for this book
is available from the British Library.

ISBN 978-1-47211-710-6 (hardback)
ISBN: 978-1-47211-714-4 (ebook)

Page design by Design23
Printed and bound in Italy by
Rotolito Lombarda SpA

Constable
is an imprint of
Constable & Robinson Ltd
100 Victoria Embankment
London EC4Y 0DY

An Hachette UK Company
www.hachette.co.uk

www.constablerobinson.com

THE VERY HUNGOVER CATERPILLAR

A Parody

Josie Lloyd & Emlyn Rees
Illustrated by Gillian Johnson

CONSTABLE • LONDON

In the gloom of
the room, a fully
dressed man lies
on the sofa.

The next morning,
the TV comes on and – ugh! –

up lurches a thirsty and very
hungover caterpillar.

He starts to look for a cure.

At 7 a.m., he has one paracetamol –
but he is still hungover.

At 8 a.m., he has two cups of sweet tea and calls in sick – but he is still hungover.

At 9 a.m., he has three slices of toast, two fizzy vitamin pills and a black coffee –

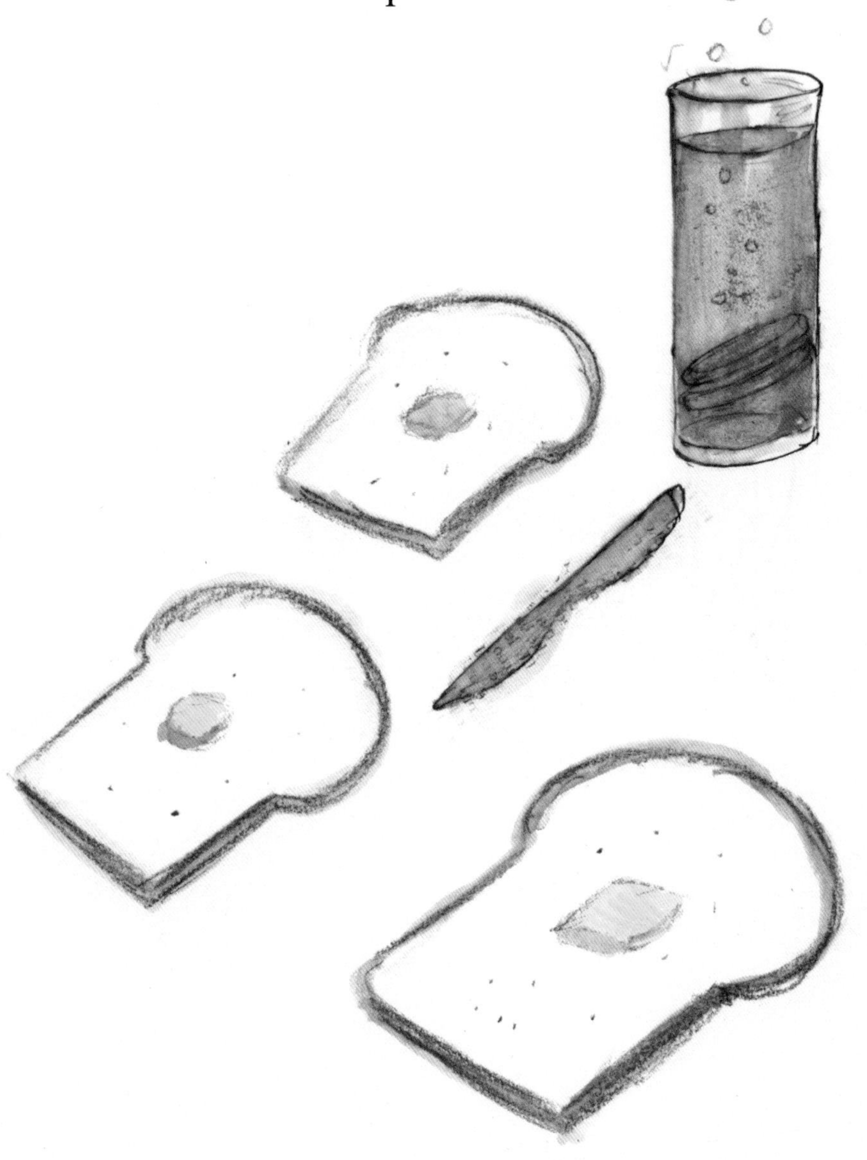

but he is still hungover.

At 11 a.m., he has four rashers of bacon, three sausages, two eggs and a slice of fried bread –

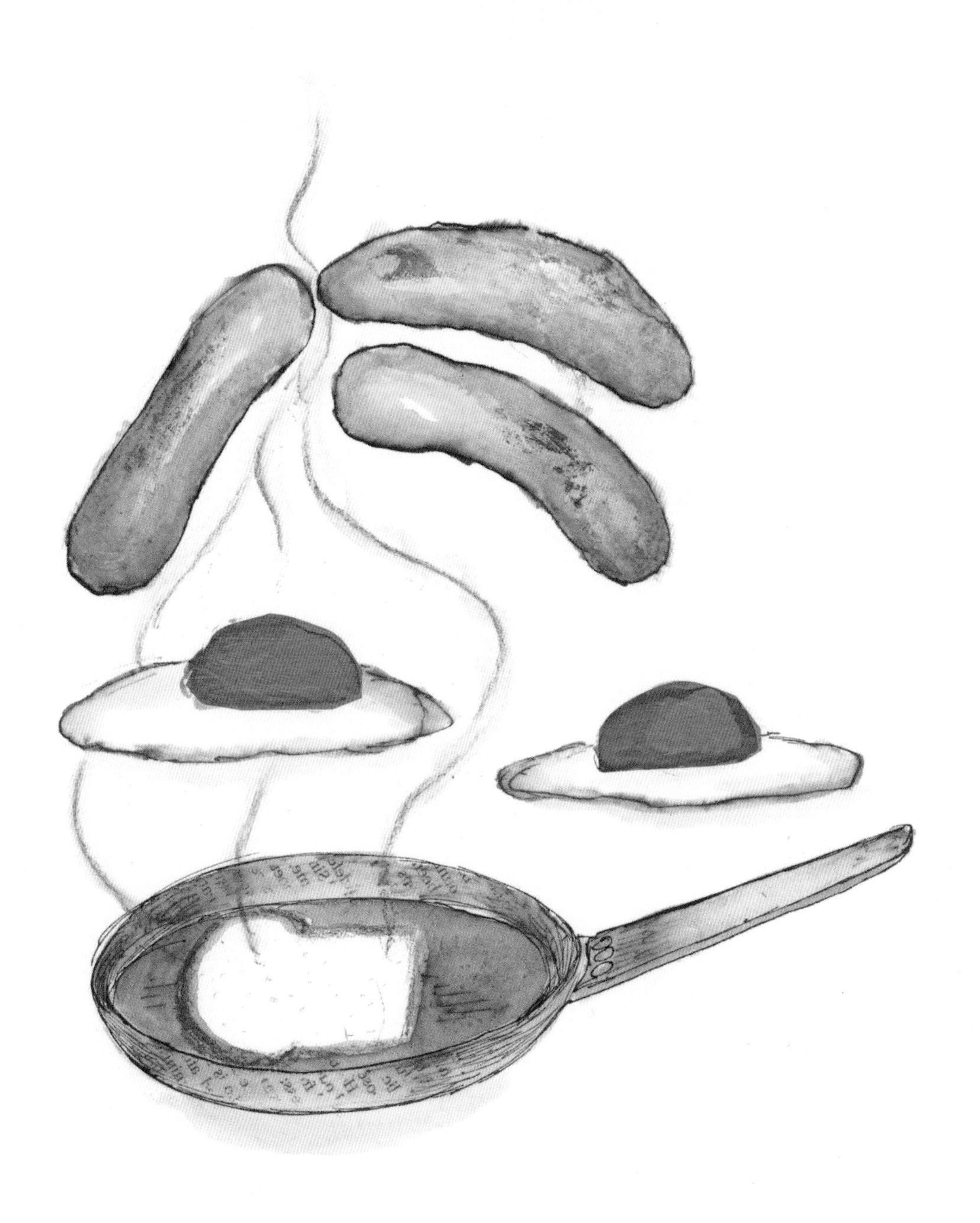

but he is still hungover.

By 4 p.m., he has watched
five hours of daytime TV,
ignored four text messages,

eaten three family-sized packets of Hula Hoops,
two Pot Noodles

and has drunk a litre bottle of full fat coke –
– but he is still hungover.

At 8 p.m., he orders one chicken tikka masala, one lamb biryani, one pilau rice …

... one tarka dhal, one aloo gobi, one onion bhaji, one naan, one chapatti, and washes it all down with one tub of double choc-chip ice-cream – but he is still hungover.

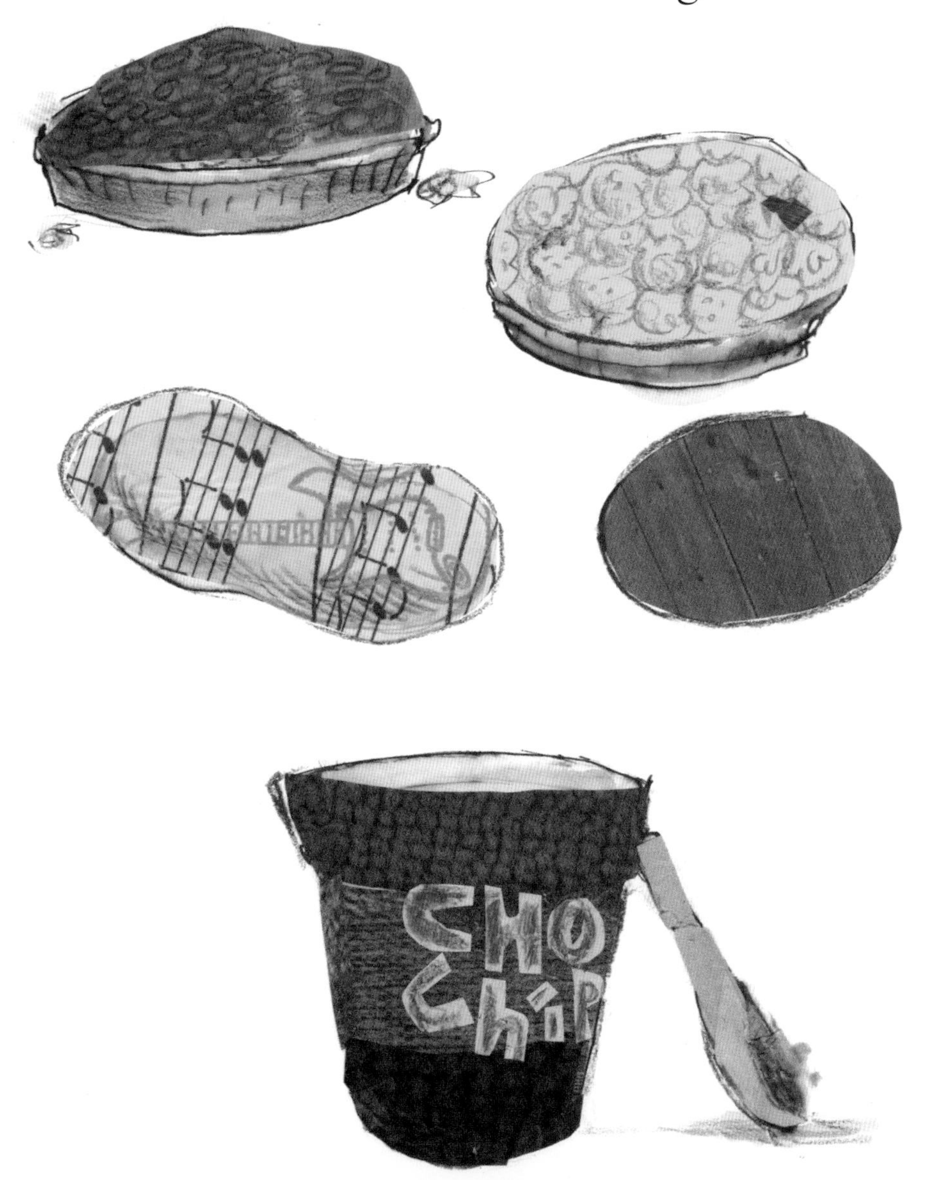

After that, he has a
massive tummyache.

Now he isn't just a hungover caterpillar anymore. He is a bloated, smelly hungover caterpillar.

He guzzles one big green bottle of indigestion medicine, does a huge burp, and feels slightly better.

He has a shave and a shower and cocoons himself inside his duvet.

He stays inside for more than twelve hours.

Then he stretches, pushes his way out,
and finally . . .

he floats
like a
butterfly!